# LNER

## SIX-COUPLED
## TENDER
## LOCOMOTIVES
## 1948–68

### ERIC SAWFORD

First published in 2006 by
Sutton Publishing Limited . Phoenix Mill
Thrupp . Stroud . Gloucestershire . GL5 2BU

British Library Cataloguing in Publication Data
A catalogue record for this book is available from the British Library.
ISBN 0-7509-4347-5

*Front endpaper*: B1 no. 61331 leaving Huntingdon in the evening sunshine with a semi-fast train.     9.61

*Back endpaper*: A3 no. 60083 *Sir Hugo* from Heaton depot approaching Huntingdon with a Glasgow express.     4.8.54

Typeset in 10/12 pt Palatino.
Typesetting and origination by
Sutton Publishing Limited.
Printed and bound in England by
J.H. Haynes & Co. Ltd, Sparkford.

# Contents

No. 61032 *Stembok*, a member of the B1 class introduced in 1942, is pictured here at Stockton.     8.7.56

No. 60050 *Persimmon* heading a Kings Cross to Peterborough service as V2 no. 60948 passes on the slow line with a long train of flat wagons. The bridge in this picture still exists, with another bridge carrying the busy A14 crossing over the top of it.

28.3.63

# Introduction

With the nationalisation of British Railways in 1948 the 'Big Four' regional railway companies ceased to exist. The second largest of these companies was the London & North Eastern region, and this book is concerned with the LNER's tender locomotives with six-coupled driving wheels in the period 1948–68. The LNER was formed in 1923 and used locomotives from seven companies that varied considerably in size. The motive power of each company was designed by its own Locomotive Superintendent. Many of these pre-Grouping engines were still in service at nationalisation and continued for a number of years under BR ownership, while others quickly became extinct. In the period 1923–48 the LNER had also introduced several excellent designs of their own.

Locomotive exchanges and trials took place in 1948 and the next two years were regarded as a review period. During this time existing designs were still being produced in the railway workshops. From the end of 1950 all new locomotives should have been BR Standard designs, but in practice the first of these did not appear until 1951 and pre-existing designs continued to be built. Indeed, the North British Locomotive Company did not complete the last Thompson B1 until April 1952. The final J72 0–6–0T was finished at Darlington in May 1951, more than half a century after this design had been introduced by the North Eastern Railway in 1898.

Locomotives with six-coupled wheels were the most numerous on British Railways, ranging from the powerful Pacifics to the huge number of 0–6–0s used on local services and goods traffic. With motive power from several railways incorporated into the LNER, it was essential to introduce a classification system. Based on wheel arrangement, and covering both tender and tank locomotives, the new system was alphabetical with numbers indicating the designs coming within each letter. A part number signified any modifications. This was important as many locomotives were rebuilt during their lifetime, including fitting Belpaire boilers, superheating, improved cabs and other changes. The new system was approved in September 1923 and introduced throughout the following year. The LNER class references are the ones used in this book; those of the pre-Grouping railways were very different. The same classification system was used for tank locomotives, which will be dealt with in a companion volume.

After Grouping the LNER took control of six principal locomotive works, all of which were still in existence at nationalisation. Two of them, Cowlairs and Inverurie, became part of the Scottish Region, as did the ex-LNER locomotives allocated to sheds north of the border. Generally engines maintained by a particular works continued to visit them when attention was required, although in due course some administrative changes occurred.

The classification of LNER locomotives commenced with the letter 'A' for 4–6–2s, which were passenger engines. The principal class consisted of thirty-four streamlined Gresley A4 Pacifics, together with seventy-eight A3s. In addition there were several Thompson & Peppercorn designs; the best known of these were the forty-nine examples of the A1 class. The sole representative of the A1/1 class was no. 60113 *Great Northern*. Originally built by Gresley and rebuilt by Thompson, these engines were a development of the original design for new construction.

The letter 'W' was used for the 4–6–4 wheel arrangement. The LNER's sole example of the class was again a passenger locomotive, W1 no. 60700. This started life as an experimental high-pressure 4-cylinder compound with water-tube boiler. Designed by

The resumption of through summer workings after the war once again brought the Haymarket A4s to London. No. 60012 *Commonwealth of Australia*, one of the engines concerned, is seen here arriving back at Haymarket depot. The coat of arms carried by this locomotive can be seen below the cabside number.                                    21.8.55

Gresley, it was introduced in 1929 and aroused much interest when it emerged from Doncaster Works. In 1937 the locomotive was rebuilt as a 3-cylinder engine with conventional boiler. Unfortunately it never quite lived up to expectations and in its later years did not appear on the most prestigious express services, which remained in the hands of the A4s. In June 1959 it was withdrawn.

Other passenger classes were the B12 4–6–0s, introduced by S.D. Holden for the Great Eastern Railway in 1911, and the 'Sandringhams', class B17, a Gresley design first introduced in 1928. Two of the Sandringhams were streamlined, although this was removed shortly after nationalisation. Several B17s were rebuilt by Thompson as 2-cylinder engines, among which was the later to be renamed *Royal Sovereign*, used for Royal train workings.

Mixed traffic locomotives were invaluable on all railway systems, and had to be equally at home on passenger, fast goods, parcels and even heavy freight trains when necessary. Gresley introduced the V2 class, a particularly famous design, in 1936. In the early stages streamlining was proposed but this was abandoned at the drawing stage. No. 60800 *Green Arrow* was completed at Doncaster in June 1936. The V2s were highly successful and well liked by enginemen, and have every right to be recorded in railway history as a 'classic' design. During the war years these engines performed many Herculean haulage feats and were often referred to as 'war-winners'. I lived near the East Coast main line at this time and I can personally recall their efforts.

Following the introduction of the V2s a second 2–6–2 design was produced at Doncaster. These were lightweight engines classified V4. Only two were in fact completed, both in 1941. No. 61700 was named *Bantam Cock*, and it was originally intended that this locomotive would be the first of a sizeable class. However, in 1941 Thompson took over as Chief Mechanical Engineer and preference was given to the B1 4–6–0 class, which eventually numbered 410 locomotives, 136 of which were built in BR days.

The letter 'K' referred to 2–6–0 designs. The oldest of these were the K2s which dated back to Great Northern Railway days, Gresley introducing them in 1914. Several K2s were fitted with side-window cabs for use on the West Highland line and elsewhere in Scotland. Thirteen of them were named, all after Scottish lochs. In the mid-1950s the highest number of K2s in the Eastern Region were to be found at Colwick, followed by Boston. The first K2 locomotive was withdrawn in 1955, and by 1960 their numbers had been dramatically reduced. Several were to end their days as stationary boilers, and it was one of these that was the last of the class to be withdrawn. The K3s were a development of the K2, with the prototype appearing in 1924. In 1945 Thompson rebuilt one as a 2-cylinder engine, with higher boiler pressure and 20x26in cylinders. BR no. 61863 was the sole example of the K5 design.

In the 1930s more powerful locomotives were required for the West Highland line and in 1937 the Gresley K4 made its debut. The six members of the class were built at Darlington in 1937–8. All were named. The first was *Loch Long*, and the other five were named after Scottish clan chiefs appropriate to the district. In 1945 Thompson rebuilt *MacCallin Mor* as a 2-cylinder locomotive and it was reclassified K1/1. I can well recall this engine working from New England to London on goods trains. After trials it moved on to Newcastle before returning north of the border. From this design Peppercorn, who had succeeded Thompson, developed his very successful K1 class. In mid-1947 the order for this seventy-strong design was placed with the North British Locomotive Company. The first was completed in May 1949, and the remainder followed in quick succession, with the last entering traffic in March 1950.

In 1948 a large number of 0–6–0s of various classes passed into British Railways stock, and the letter 'J' was used for the considerable number of them originating from pre-Grouping companies. Ivatt designed the J1 class for the Great Northern Railway. With their 5ft 8in driving wheels, these engines were introduced principally to work fast goods on the main line but their suitability for passenger trains was soon discovered and they were often to be found on such duties. Some forty-three years later the last survivor, no. 65013 of

A1 no. 60123 *H A Ivatt* leaving Huntingdon with a Peterborough semi-fast. This engine was allocated to Ardsley depot at the time, although in its final years it spent some time at Copley Hill. In 1962 no. 60123 was involved in an accident, just a few miles south at Offord, which resulted in its withdrawal. It was the first A1 to be condemned. 5.7.54

Hitchin shed, took over a fourteen-coach Leeds express and worked the train unaided through to Kings Cross. This locomotive was normally to be seen on much more mundane duties, frequently working engineers' trains to Connington tip and elsewhere on the main line. No. 65013 was withdrawn in November 1954.

As with the earlier J1 class, only a small number of J2s were built. In all ten were constructed at Doncaster in 1912. H.A. Ivatt designed them for mixed traffic work, although here again they were frequently used on passenger duties, notably on excursion trains. The first member of the class was withdrawn in 1946 but the remaining engines passed into British Railways ownership. Another was withdrawn in 1950, followed by six in 1953, and the two survivors ended their days in January and July 1954.

The oldest Great Northern Railway 0–6–0s to be taken into British Railways stock were the J3 and J4s, the former being rebuilds of the latter. Much of the work entrusted to these engines in their final years was on engineers' trains and local pick-up goods. The last two J4s were New England engines which were withdrawn in 1951. One of them, no. 64112, built at Doncaster in 1896, was a fairly common sight on the main line heading engineers' trains to Connington tip. However, when traffic was not busy this veteran locomotive was given the main line with a heavy train. In 1952 the remaining rebuilt J3s were reduced by over half, with the final example being withdrawn in 1954.

In the early years following nationalisation New England depot was home to a large number of ex-Great Northern Railway 0–6–0s. The most numerous were the J6s, with just under a third of the stock to be found there. Many brickyards were active in the area and J6s were frequently to be seen on trip working; they were also widely used on the Midland and Great Northern railways. In 1950 the depot also had seven J3s, five J4s and four J1s.

In the early 1900s the continual increase in coal and goods traffic generally resulted in the need for additional locomotives to help handle this work. H.A. Ivatt introduced the J5 class in 1908. These engines were constructed to basically the same dimensions as the earlier J1s but with 5ft 2in driving wheels instead of 5ft 8in. In all twenty were built at Doncaster in 1909–10. In their final years one of the best places to see the remaining J5s was Colwick, but all were withdrawn by 1955.

The final class of Great Northern Railway 0–6–0s was the J6; 110 were built between 1911 and 1922, all at Doncaster Works. The original design was by H.A. Ivatt, and when he retired in 1911 Nigel Gresley took over. During the following years slight modifications were introduced. On many occasions the J6s could also be seen on passenger trains. They were very useful locomotives, well liked by enginemen. During the 1950s they were most often found on local goods, and in their final years on engineers' trains, replacing earlier ex-GNR 0–6–0s. Withdrawal did not commence until 1955 and it was to be another three years before serious inroads into the class were made. The final examples were withdrawn in 1962.

Although the Great Eastern Railway operated in an area not noted for heavy industry, much of its traffic was in some way connected to agriculture or the transport of coal for industrial and domestic purposes. In the early years the main goods locomotives in this region were the J15 class 0–6–0s, with 272 being built between 1883 and 1913. These were powerful engines for their size and capable of Herculean effort when the need arose. On one occasion the Huntingdon pilot, a Cambridge J15, was called upon to take over a heavy eleven-coach express after its original A4 engine failed. The gallant J15 (power classification 2F) managed to work as far as Hitchin, where it was relieved by a V2 commandeered from a goods train. Many of the J15s were steam brake only, but those equipped to work passenger services were still doing so well into the 1950s. Cambridge had a number of these in its allocation, their regular duties including the Mildenhall services, the Colne Valley line and a daily working through to Kettering. For many years the latter was the domain of no. 65390, built in 1890; only when the engine required maintenance or a works visit did one of the others take over. This particular engine was fitted with an extra lamp bracket on its buffer beam to bring it in line with LMR practice.

Hitchin depot had in its allocation E4 2–4–0 no. 62785 and J15 0–6–0 no. 65479, which were used principally to work leave trains from RAF Henlow. When not engaged on this work they

The smokebox door shows signs of hard work on A3 no. 60063 *Isinglass*, seen here heading a semi-fast at Huntingdon. This locomotive was allocated to Kings Cross at the time, moving to New England in October 1963. A number of A3s were to end their days at this depot, working to London and York.                              14.4.63

also carried out other duties, especially the J15. On a number of occasions I saw this engine working heavy engineers' trains on the main line to Connington tip. Given a clear road, especially if on the main line, it took the 1-in-200 climb north of Huntingdon in its stride.

The J15 was a straightforward design with a low axle loading, which enabled the class to work over lines where larger engines were not permitted. One of these was between St Ives and Huntingdon East, where the wooden trestle bridge had both weight and speed restrictions. In all, 127 examples passed into British Railways ownership, perhaps not surprisingly, as in 1923 the J15 was the most numerous class. It was not until 1962 that the last few were withdrawn, among them a steam brake engine built at Stratford Works in 1889.

The next 0–6–0 to appear on the Great Eastern Railway was a powerful design with a round-topped firebox and a sizeable side-window cab. Introduced by J. Holden in 1900, they were to become the LNER J16 (later rebuilt as class J17). All were constructed at Stratford Works. All ninety built were taken into LNER stock, with all but one passing into British Railways ownership. That one had been extensively damaged by a German V2 rocket in 1944. During the 1950s you could find J17s throughout eastern England. Some were equipped to work passenger stock. Other than the engine already mentioned, the class remained intact until 1954. From 1958 onwards withdrawals commenced at a steadily increasing rate, although a number survived into the 1960s, with the last of the class being withdrawn in 1962. Some J17s ended their days on steam-heating work, such as no. 65541 of March depot.

In 1912 another 0–6–0 was to appear on the Great Eastern, designed by the new Locomotive Superintendent A.J. Hill. In all, thirty-five were built, all at Stratford Works. The first examples were classified J18, but were rebuilt during LNER days as J19s. All thirty-five of these engines passed into British Railways ownership. During the early 1950s the March engines were

Signs of hard work are readily apparent on the smokebox door of J37 no. 64606, photographed at St Margaret's depot. During the 1950s some twenty-nine members of the class were allocated here, although a number were always out-stationed at sub-sheds within its control.                    21.8.55

frequently to be seen on the St Ives loop line hauling heavy coal trains and return empties. Withdrawals commenced in the late 1950s, with the last being condemned in 1962.

The final 0–6–0 design for the Great Eastern Railway, the J20, appeared just three years before Grouping. Again A.J. Hill was responsible for what proved to be the most powerful 0–6–0 to run in Britain, a distinction held until the introduction of the austere O.V. Bulleid Q1 in 1942. March was one of the depots to have a long association with these engines, not just in its own allocation but also in terms of visitors. During the early to mid-1950s J20s were regularly used on London freights, although later WDs took over much of this work. The thirty-five-strong class was still intact in January 1948 and it was not until January 1959 that the first J20 was withdrawn. In 1960–1 their numbers were decimated and the last four, all March engines, were withdrawn in September 1962. They had stood idle in the yards for several months in company with several K3s and a solitary J17, which ended its days as a stationary boiler.

As might be expected, the North Eastern Railway had a huge number of 0–6–0s for the busy coal and other mineral traffic in the area. In the mid-1880s the railway had been in urgent need of additional goods locomotives. Following his success with the J15 design for the Great Eastern Railway, T.W. Worsdell, who by this time had taken over on the North Eastern Railway, produced the J21 class 0–6–0s. His J15s had been highly successful but the J21s were even more so, the increased power no doubt proving welcome on the often steeply graded routes in the north-east. The first examples emerged from Gateshead Works in 1886. Between 1886 and 1895 a total of 201 were constructed, all at Gateshead except for the thirty that were Darlington engines. Some were built as compounds, others as simples, but the former were eventually rebuilt in 1901–13 to conform with the latter.

While the J21 design was principally intended for goods traffic, a considerable number of these locomotives were equipped for working passenger stock. They could, at times, also be seen in various parts of the north-east on local and excursion trains, but they will probably be best remembered for the Darlington to Penrith and Tebay route with its formidable climb over Stainmore. And they didn't only work passenger services on this route – they could also be seen here on heavy mineral trains. In 1948 eighty-three examples passed into British Railways ownership, and more than thirty of them were condemned in the next few years. The last survivor of this once sizeable class was not withdrawn until 1962.

In 1890 T.W. Worsdell retired as Locomotive Superintendent on health grounds. The position was taken by his brother William, who remained in the post for twenty years. During this time he introduced a number of excellent designs, including the J25 class. Others included the D20 4–4–0s and the J72 0–6–0Ts, which made their debut in 1898 and proved to be a very useful design. Indeed, they led to the construction of further engines in British Railways days.

What was to become the LNER J24 was introduced in 1894, and seventy were built. Those that were taken into BR stock were withdrawn in the next two or three years. In 1904 the J26 class made its debut. During 1904–5 fifty were constructed at Darlington and Gateshead Works. They were designed to handle the constantly increasing loads on goods trains. Locomotives of this class were easily distinguished by the large-diameter boiler fitted. These were steam brake engines, and all passed into British Railways ownership. Withdrawals commenced in 1958, but twenty-five were still in service at the start of the 1960s, the last survivor going in 1962. The J26s proved to be a long-lived and very useful class, all completing over fifty years' service.

In 1906 Worsdell introduced another long-lived class of 0–6–0s, the J27s, 115 of which were constructed. Darlington built sixty-five of them, with the rest being produced by three private companies, Beyer Peacock, Robert Stephenson and the North British Locomotive Company. The J27's tractive effort was the same as the earlier J26's; here again all were fitted with steam brake only and worked coal trains. The entire class was taken over by British Railways. The two Blyth sheds had a long association with these engines, and even as late as 1965 thirty-six examples were to be found in the area.

During 1900 J.G. Robinson was appointed Locomotive Superintendent of the Great Central Railway, a position he was to hold until 1922. Unquestionably one of his finest designs was the 04 class 2–8–0, a true 'classic' in railway history. In 1901 he introduced a new 0–6–0 which became the LNER class J11. Between 1901 and 1910 a total of 174 were built. The first batch was produced by Neilson Reed & Company, and others followed from Beyer Peacock, the Vulcan Foundry and the Yorkshire Engine Company; the last fifty-eight were constructed at Gorton Works. Many locomotive designs received odd nicknames, and the J11s were no exception, becoming known as 'Pom Poms'. The J11's sharp exhaust beat sounded very similar to the quick-firing gun of that name used in the recent South African conflict. Although built as goods locomotives, the J11s were not unknown on passenger services, especially in the Manchester and Sheffield areas. Over the years they were to be found at other depots outside their normal territory. All members of the class passed into British Railways ownership. Withdrawals commenced in 1954, and a considerable number survived into the 1960s; the last J11 was condemned in 1962, a year that saw the extinction of many famous designs.

In 1897 the Manchester, Sheffield & Lincolnshire Railway changed its name to the Great Central. Five years earlier, in 1892, the Locomotive Superintendent T. Parker had introduced a new 0–6–0 design, which was to continue being constructed during the terms of office of both H. Pollitt and J.G. Robinson. Some sixty-six engines were built by Beyer Peacock in 1896–7, while one other private builder, Kitson & Company, built another twelve. The locomotive works at Gorton constructed forty more in two batches. The class eventually totalled 124, seventy-eight of which made it into BR days. These engines were designed for goods traffic but, as with many other classes, they were not unknown on passenger services, especially in the Manchester area. Withdrawal of the locomotives that passed into British Railways hands started in 1952 and continued at a steady rate through

In the mid-1950s York had sizeable allocations of both J25 and J27 class locomotives. By 1964 only the J27s remained and these were down to single figures; all were steam brake engines. No. 65844 was in good external condition. Built by Beyer Peacock & Company in August 1908, it remained in service until December 1965. 23.9.56

The twenty-five-strong J19 class comprised ten examples built as J18s, the remaining fifteen being constructed as J19s. In Gresley's day all were rebuilt as J19/2s, making them similar in many ways to the well-known J39s introduced in 1926. No. 64650 of Stratford shed is seen here at St Ives, heading for March with a long train of coal empties. 17.3.54

the 1950s. Only four made it to the 1960s, with the last two survivors going in 1961. The last MS&LR locomotive in service was no. 65157, which had been completed in January 1897.

In 1923 the North British Railway had become part of the LNER. It boasted an extensive fleet of 0–6–0s for coal and general traffic. The oldest class to make it into BR service was the J36, introduced by M. Holmes in 1888. A total of 168 were built, mostly at Cowlairs, with thirty equally divided between Neilson & Company and Sharp, Stewart & Company. Construction of the class took place over an extended period, from 1888 to 1900.

During the First World War the Railway Operating Division urgently needed locomotives for use in France, and to this end engines were commandeered from several companies. In 1917 the North British sent twenty-five J36 engines, all of which returned in 1919. When they re-entered service, the North British decided to name them after famous generals and military landmarks. As with other locomotives of this Scottish company, the names were painted on the splashers. The J36 was still a familiar sight in many parts of Scotland during the 1950s as 123 had passed into British Railways stock. Indeed, a surprising number were still in service in the 1960s, with the last survivors being withdrawn in 1966.

In 1903 W.P. Reid took up the position of Locomotive Superintendent with the North British Railway. Shortly afterwards it was decided that there was a requirement for more powerful locomotives to handle the increasing traffic and heavier loads involved, as on other railways. As a result the J35 class was introduced in 1906. Construction took place at the North British Locomotive Company, with the Atlas, Queens Park and Hyde Park Works all involved. Over the years the company's own works added thirty-six to the grand total of seventy-six. When British Railways came into existence in 1948, all but six of the J35 class were still in service.

The final development of the 0–6–0s by the North British Railway was the J37; these were a superheated development of the J35, with increased cylinder diameter. Over the period 1914–21 a total of 104 were built at Cowlairs and by the North British Locomotive Company. These powerful locomotives were well liked by enginemen. The whole class passed into British Railways ownership and remained intact until 1959. During the 1950s their main duties were on trip workings and local goods. One shed that had a long association with both the J35s and the J37s was St Margaret's, Edinburgh, the largest depot in the Scottish Region. In the mid-1950s it had an allocation of 220 engines, including sixteen J35s and twenty-nine J37s. One sub-shed, Seafield, had a regular allocation of six of each class. By contrast the two Aberdeen depots, Kittybrewster and Ferryhill, had just one J35 each. The J37s were a long-lived design; all passed into BR stock and it was not until 1959 that the first locomotive was withdrawn. They became extinct in 1966.

Nigel Gresley introduced many famous designs on the LNER during his long period in office. Rather surprisingly, it was two J38 0–6–0s that had the distinction of being the last Gresley engines in service. In all there were thirty-five J38s; all were built in 1926 at Darlington in a six-month period. In LNER and BR days much of the J38s' work was handling coal traffic in Scotland. The first locomotive was withdrawn at the end of 1962, with the last example going in April 1967.

Later in 1926 Gresley introduced the J39. This would become a much larger class, totalling 289. Construction took place over a long period of time, with the final locomotive being completed in August 1941. All were built at Darlington Works except for twenty-eight built by Beyer Peacock in 1936–7. The J39s were very similar in appearance to the J38s, one difference being the size of the driving wheels, which on the J39s was 5ft 2in, as opposed to the J38's 4ft 8in. The J39s had a wide distribution, including some in Scotland, and their principal duties were on goods trains, although they could occasionally be seen on passenger services. With increasing numbers of diesels becoming available work was reduced for the J39s, as it was for many classes. In 1959 withdrawals started, and increased at an alarming rate; the last J39 was withdrawn at the end of 1962.

As mentioned earlier, after nationalisation the BR Standard designs followed. Many of these were six-coupled, but they fall outside the scope of this book.

Running on clear signals on a bitterly cold February day, A4 no. 60007 *Sir Nigel Gresley* was going in fine style with 'The Heart of Midlothian'. No. 60007 was one of the 'top link' Kings Cross A4s. The single chimney was replaced with a double chimney in December 1957.

26.2.54

# Chapter 1
# Passenger Locomotives

There were three work classifications in use for steam locomotives in British Railways days, passenger (P), mixed traffic (MT) and freight (F). However, this was by no means a hard and fast rule, as will be seen from examples of passenger locomotives at work on other duties. In addition, all engines were given a power rating which preceded the relevant letter. The famous Gresley streamlined Pacifics, for example, were classed 8P. Among the mixed traffic engines are some classes that many would expect to find in the passenger category, which was their usual work. The Thompson & Peppercorn Pacifics of class A2 were all classified as mixed traffic.

When considering the former LNER locomotives in the passenger category, one class stands head and shoulders above the rest. The world-famous Gresley A4 class streamlined Pacifics were, without doubt, a classic design and among the finest passenger steam locomotives ever built. Introduced in 1935, these engines soon achieved excellent results. One highlight came when *Mallard* attained the world speed record for a steam locomotive. Then came the war, which changed everything. In due course the A4s, along with other designs, appeared in black livery. After a period of recovery, in which both track and locomotive maintenance was brought up to date, the A4s took charge of the non-stop services between Edinburgh and London, with Kings Cross and Haymarket depots sharing the work. Right up to the closure to steam of Kings Cross (or 'Top Shed' as it was known), the A4s were always to be seen in immaculate condition.

A4 no. 60003 *Andrew K. McCosh* speeds through Huntingdon with the Tees-Tyne Pullman. This engine was originally named *Osprey*, but was renamed in 1942. It received a double chimney in July 1957. No. 60003 was a Kings Cross 'top link' locomotive for many years, right up to withdrawal in December 1962. It ended its days where it started, at Doncaster Works.                                                                                        26.4.54

(*Opposite, top*): The fireman had a chance to take things easy on the 1-in-200 descent from Abbots Ripton. Here no. 60029 *Woodcock* has just passed Huntingdon on its way to London with the 'Flying Scotsman'. This engine was still fitted with a single chimney, but received the double type in October 1958.                                                             28.4.54

(*Opposite, bottom*): Only once do I recall seeing an A4 on a heavy coal train. New England depot normally provided a Standard 9F or WD 2–8–0 for this duty, but presumably a motive power shortage had resulted in A4 no. 60014 *Silver Link* being used on this occasion. It is seen here approaching Huntingdon, the low evening light picking out details on the locomotive.                                                                                                                     12.6.57

At many of the larger depots it was not unusual to find locomotives under repair standing in the yard because space in repair shops was limited. This is A4 no. 60032 *Gannet*, a Kings Cross engine, at Doncaster shed. This locomotive received a double chimney in 1958.                    10.11.54

Two of Haymarket's immaculate A4s ready for their next turn of duty. On the right is the well-known no. 60009 *Union of South Africa*, still awaiting the return of one of its burnished buffers. The other engine is no. 60004 *William Whitelaw*. No one would have thought at this time that over fifty years later no. 60009 would be still active on the main line.                    22.8.55

A4 no. 60006 *Sir Ralph Wedgwood* pulls away from Huntingdon with a Sunday semi-fast from Kings Cross to Grantham. Built in 1938, it was originally named *Herring Gull* but was renamed in January 1944. For many years a Kings Cross engine, it ended its days at Aberdeen Ferryhill. It was cut up at Wishaw, having been withdrawn in September 1965. 27.1.53

A4 no. 60012 *Commonwealth of Australia* was another of the Haymarket 'top link' A4s. Seen here at its home shed, it still has a single chimney; it received a double chimney three years later. Its final years were spent at Aberdeen Ferryhill, from where it was withdrawn in August 1964. After a period in store it was cut up at Wishaw. 21.8.55

No. 60006 *Sir Ralph Wedgwood*, photographed at Huntingdon on a dismal grey afternoon with a northbound express.
21.2.62

The long climb to Abbots Ripton was having little effect on A4 no. 60033 *Seagull*, heading a Kings Cross to Newcastle service. This was another of the 'top link' A4s and, as can be seen, it was in fine condition. Surprisingly it was withdrawn later the same month.
4.10.62

Sunday engineering work on the main line often resulted in trains using the slow lines. This was the case with A4 no. 60006 *Sir Ralph Wedgwood*, seen here passing Huntingdon. The bottom front smokebox casing had been damaged; note the large dent. 2.10.55

The 9.16 a.m. service from Huntingdon ran non-stop to Kings Cross and was usually headed by a Kings Cross engine working back. Here A4 no. 60033 *Seagull* pulls away on a grey morning. This engine was fitted with a double chimney from new in 1938. It was among the first A4s to be withdrawn (the very first was one that had been badly damaged in an air raid in 1942). 1.8.54

Diesel locomotives were becoming increasingly common on the East Coast main line in the early 1960s. Despite this, the stud of Kings Cross A4s were still in fine condition, as demonstrated by the immaculate no. 60008 *Dwight D. Eisenhower*, seen here heading the Yorkshire Pullman. This fine locomotive was later to cross the Atlantic for preservation in the United States. 9.61

(*Opposite, top*): I was fortunate enough to travel on the A4 Preservation Society special to Weymouth with no. 60024 *Kingfisher* in charge. The locomotive gave us splendid runs in both directions, especially so on the return to Waterloo. No. 60024 was allocated to Aberdeen at the time but it was there for only a short period. Withdrawal was six months away when this picture was taken at Weymouth shed. 26.3.66

(*Opposite, bottom*): A4 no. 60024 *Kingfisher* was one of seven A4 locomotives allocated to Haymarket during the 1950s. It moved to St Margaret's in 1963 and spent its final months of service at Aberdeen. 26.3.66

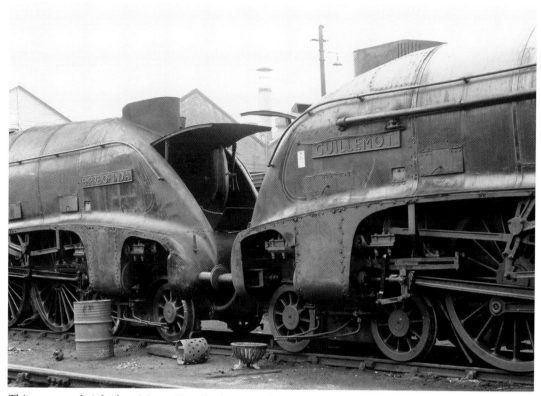

This was a sad sight for visitors. Time had run out for both these A4s and within a few weeks they fell victim to the scrapman's cutting torch. Surprisingly the nameplates were still in place on both these engines. Both had been allocated in the north, no. 60011 *Empire of India* at Haymarket and no. 60020 *Guillemot* at Gateshead.          2.5.64

For a number of years no. 60020 *Guillemot* was a Gateshead engine. Withdrawn two months earlier, it was sent to Darlington Works, where it was cut up a short time after this picture was taken.      2.5.64

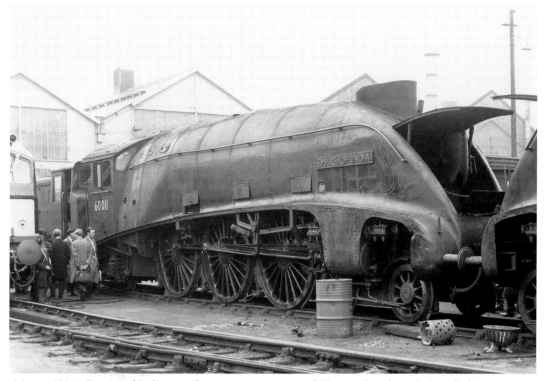

A4 no. 60011 *Empire of India* was for many years one of Haymarket depot's 'top link' passenger locomotives, although in its final years it was transferred to Aberdeen. It is seen here at Darlington Works, from where it was withdrawn in May 1964. It was cut up a short time later. 2.5.64

The A4s worked 'The Elizabethan' for the last time in 1961. It should have been the previous year, but owing to the lack of diesel engines steam enjoyed one more year in charge. A4 no. 60009 *Union of South Africa* had just arrived with the non-stop and was being coaled in the service area that was near the station in those days. 9.61

A4 no. 60033 *Seagull* stands ready at Kings Cross to join its train, the Tees-Tyne Pullman. This was another of the Kings Cross 'top link' A4s. This engine was one of those that took part in the 1948 locomotive exchanges, giving an outstanding performance on the Western Region.    9.61

(*Opposite, top*): A3 no. 60090 *Grand Parade* had evidently run hot, as the rear set of driving wheels has been removed. The engine was photographed at St Margaret's, its home depot being Haymarket. *Grand Parade* was for a number of years allocated to depots in the southern section of the LNER, moving back north of the border permanently in 1950.    21.8.55

(*Opposite, bottom*): Four A3s were allocated to Carlisle Canal depot. No. 60079 *Bayardo*, pictured here at Haymarket, was one of them. The others were *Sir Visto*, *Coronach* and *Flamingo*. Enthusiasts had little chance of seeing these four engines south of Peterborough, even after a works visit.    21.8.55

The Darlington Pacifics spent some of their time as stand-by locomotives to cover main line failures, and this is A3 no. 60071 *Tranquil* on precisely that duty. This engine was one of the batch of twenty built in 1924 by the North British Locomotive Company. The remaining members of the class were all built at Doncaster.                                    7.7.56

Immediately after Huntingdon station, the main line faces a long 1-in-200 climb but it presented no problem for A3 no. 60110 *Robert the Devil*, seen here going in fine style with a Newcastle express. This engine was completed in July 1923 and withdrawn in May 1963.                                    18.6.57

It is of course widely known that only one A3 made it into preservation, the legendary no. 60103 *Flying Scotsman*. It is seen here at Darlington shed just over a year after purchase, resplendent in LNER green livery, having worked the 'London North Eastern Flier' and carrying its pre-nationalisation number 4472. The first section was worked by classmate no. 60106 *Flying Fox*.                                                     2.5.64

A3s arriving at Doncaster Works for general overhaul were usually in a run-down condition. No. 60043 *Brown Jack* was a Haymarket engine. In February 1959 it received a double chimney and in February 1962 smoke deflectors. This engine was the last of the class to be built. Completed in February 1935 at Doncaster, it was withdrawn in May 1964.     23.9.56

Even in the 1950s the legendary no. 60103 *Flying Scotsman* was often called upon to work enthusiasts' specials, in this case one composed of Gresley stock. Here this grand engine approaches Huntingdon with a Westminster Bank Railway Society Special to York. No. 60103 was a Grantham engine for most of the 1950s, moving to Kings Cross at the end of 1957. It remained there until withdrawal, when it was purchased for preservation. 3.4.55

Pacifics from the Newcastle depots were occasional visitors south of Peterborough. Here A3 no. 60083 *Sir Hugo* of Heaton depot is trying to make up time as it approaches Huntingdon with the late-running Glasgow express. 4.8.54

Gateshead A3 no. 60042 *Singapore* was in poor external condition when photographed at Heaton. This engine spent most of its working life in the North Eastern Region until the 1960s, when it moved north of the border and spent short periods at Aberdeen and St Margaret's.                    7.7.56

Certain names tend to stick in one's memory. One that sticks in mine was no. 60098 *Spion Kop*, which was named after the winner of the 1920 Derby. I can well remember it as a Kings Cross engine, before it moved north of the border in 1950. It is seen here arriving at Perth depot, having worked in from Edinburgh.                    25.8.55

During the 1950s Darlington usually had two A3s in its allocation, although they weren't always the same two. Here no. 60076 *Galopin* stands ready for duty, between two tank locomotives that had been through works for a general overhaul.   7.7.56

A3 no. 60099 *Call Boy* was named after the winner of the 1927 Derby. This locomotive was completed in April 1930 at Doncaster Works and remained in service until October 1963. For many years it was allocated to Haymarket. After a period in store it was cut up in July 1964 by Arnott Young.   8.7.56

The LNER named many of the A3 class after famous racehorses. No. 60071 *Tranquil* was named after the winner of the 1923 St Leger and the 1000 Guineas. Originally LNER no. 2570, it became no. 71 in 1946 and ultimately BR 60071. Note the works plate, which had been modified to read 71.

7.7.56

For some years A3 no. 60102 *Sir Frederick Banbury* was allocated to Neasden and worked on Great Central services; it was one of a very small number of A3s not to receive smoke deflectors. It moved to Kings Cross in December 1960. It is seen here at Huntingdon heading an Edinburgh fast goods. Just two months after this picture was taken it was withdrawn.

14.9.61

For a number of years A3 no. 60036 *Colombo* was allocated to Leeds Neville Hill shed. In 1964 it moved to Darlington, where this picture was taken. Time was running out for the A3s, and many had already been withdrawn by this time. No. 60036 was to follow in six months, ending its days at Drapers of Hull.                                                                  2.5.64

(*Opposite, top*): In their final years A3s from New England depot were frequent visitors to York. No. 60112 *St Simon* is seen here in poor external condition, the grime obscuring the crest on the tender. Very little cleaning was done on steam locomotives in the 1960s, except for those chosen to work specials.                                                         2.5.64

(*Opposite, bottom*): In their final days the Eastern Region A3s were in a very run-down condition. No. 60050 *Persimmon* is seen here leaving Huntingdon with a local passenger service. This A3's last two months in service were spent at New England in company with several other members of the class.                                                              28.3.63

For many years Darlington shed kept a Pacific locomotive on stand-by to take over on expresses at short notice. This is A3 no. 60045 *Lemburg* on this duty. This engine received its double chimney in October 1959 and the smoke deflectors in November 1962. Just two years later it was withdrawn, ending its days at Drapers scrapyard, Hull.                2.5.64

(*Opposite, top*): The first Sunday Kings Cross to Grantham semi-fast was worked by either a Kings Cross or a Grantham engine. A3 no. 60056 *Centenary* was nearing the end of its days, being withdrawn six months after this picture was taken. After a period in store at Doncaster it was cut up in November 1963.                14.4.63

(*Opposite, bottom*): A3 no. 60106 *Flying Fox* was the centre of attention at Peterborough, having arrived with the 'London North Eastern Flier'. This engine was allocated to New England depot at this time. It was withdrawn in December 1964 and ended its days at Kings scrapyard, Norwich.                2.5.64

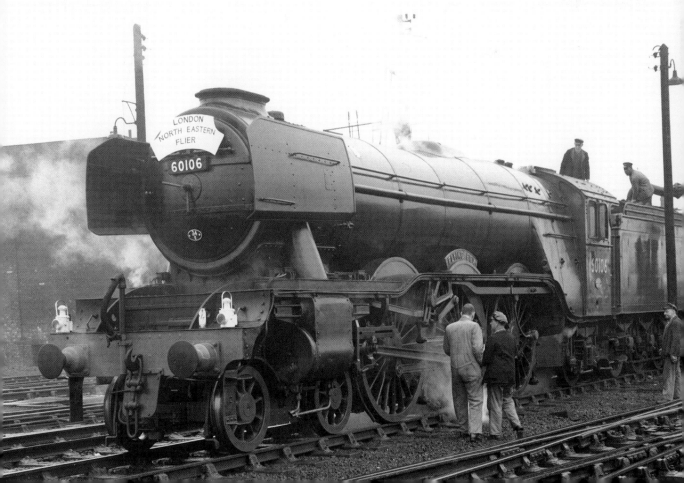

A1/1 no. 60113 *Great Northern* departs from Huntingdon amid clouds of steam with a Grantham to London special. In 1945 Edward Thompson rebuilt this engine from class A10. No. 60113 was allocated to Grantham at the time this picture was taken. In 1957 it was transferred to Doncaster, where it ended its working days, being withdrawn in December 1962.                                                                                                10.10.54

(*Opposite, top*): The Peppercorn A1s were a regular sight on the East Coast main line. Well liked by enginemen, they were powerful locomotives capable of a fair turn of speed. Despite this, they were somewhat overshadowed by the Gresley A4s. Here no. 60158 *Aberdonian*, allocated to Doncaster at the time, leaves Huntingdon with a semi-fast.   14.3.63

(*Opposite, bottom*): During the mid-1950s no A1s were allocated to Kings Cross, although they were of course daily visitors. At this time Grantham had eleven A1s in its allocation, and many express trains used to change engines there. Here no. 60149 *Amadis* heads a heavy express just south of Huntingdon.                                                                        20.2.54

A1 no. 60138 *Boswell* makes a spirited stand from Huntingdon. This engine was allocated to York depot for several years and was withdrawn from there in September 1965, ending its days at Wards of Killmarsh, which was responsible for cutting up several A1s.

24.2.63

(*Opposite, top*): A1 no. 60138 *Boswell* stands on the ash pits at York. This engine spent its final years allocated to this depot, from where it was withdrawn in September 1965. After a short period in store it was sent to Wards of Killamarsh for scrap.

2.5.64

(*Opposite, bottom*): A1 no. 60122 *Curlew* heads south near Huntingdon with the 'Queen of Scots' Pullman service. Although they were excellent engines, well capable of fast running and popular with enginemen, the A1s never seemed to receive the same attention from enthusiasts as the Gresley A4 Pacifics. No. 60122 was withdrawn from Doncaster in November 1962 and cut up in the works.

5.7.54

Grantham depot A1 no. 60157 *Great Eastern* pulls away from Huntingdon for Kings Cross with a special train. Five A1s of the last batch built at Doncaster in 1949, including *Great Eastern*, were fitted with Timken roller bearings. This increased the length of time between heavy repairs. Despite the success, no more A1s received roller bearings. No. 60157 was withdrawn from Doncaster shed in January 1965 and cut up by Drapers of Hull the same year.                    1.8.54

Another picture of A1 no. 60157 *Great Eastern* taken almost ten years later at York. It was still a Doncaster engine, although it had spent several years at Kings Cross during this time. No. 60157 was withdrawn in January 1965, ending its days at Drapers of Hull.                    2.5.64

The Peppercorn A1s were powerful locomotives capable of working the heaviest main line services. No. 60150 *Willbrook*, a Gateshead engine, is seen here at Haymarket. A1s from Gateshead and Heaton were also seen on occasion in London. 21.8.55

In its final years W1 4–6–4 no. 60700 was a Doncaster engine and was often used on a Kings Cross turn returning from London at 3.50 p.m. It is seen here at Huntingdon on this duty. Sir Nigel Gresley rebuilt the engine in 1937 from the experimental high-pressure 4-cylinder compound with water-tube boiler. Withdrawal came in June 1959. 2.5.55

The March parcels train arriving at St Ives behind B17 'Sandringham' no. 61619 *Welbeck Abbey*. On this occasion the train was heavily loaded. Several different locomotive types were used on this duty, including D16 4–4–0s, K3 2–6–0s and J17 0–6–0s.                                                                                                23.6.57

(*Opposite, top*): Cambridge depot had a number of 'Sandringhams' in its allocation, including no. 61624 *Lumley Castle*. The first withdrawal of the class took place in 1952, followed by two more in 1953, including *Lumley Castle*. It was to be five more years before any further withdrawals were made; thereafter the rate speeded up and the last example went in 1960.                                                                                                28.6.52

(*Opposite, bottom*): March's allocation included eleven 'Sandringhams', among them no. 61627 *Aske Hall*, seen here at Cambridge ready to leave with a local train. The building in the background was the locomotive depot. Movements on and off the shed could be easily seen from the platform end.                                                                                                10.2.55

Despite receiving a general overhaul at Doncaster Works, 'Sandringham' no. 61609 *Quidenham* only remained in service until June 1958. Heavy inroads were made into the class in 1958–9. Just sixteen remained in 1960, and all were scrapped in August that year. 23.9.56

(*Opposite, top*): Ten 'Sandringham' locomotives were rebuilt by Edward Thompson as 2-cylinder engines with 100A boilers. No. 61617 *Ford Castle*, seen here at Cambridge, was rebuilt in December 1946 and fitted with a North Eastern ex-C7 class tender. This engine was the reserve royal engine. 23.6.57

(*Opposite, bottom*): The 'Pride of Cambridge', B2 no. 61671 *Royal Sovereign*, is prepared for its next duty. When not required for royal train duties, this engine was often seen on Liverpool Street and Kings Cross services. Originally named *Manchester City*, it was renamed in 1946. It was the only B2 to run with a group-standard tender. After the withdrawal of no. 61671 in September 1958, another B2, no. 61632 *Belvoir Castle*, took over and was itself renamed *Royal Sovereign*. However, it was only a short-lived role, as it was withdrawn in February 1959. 14.11.51

Ipswich depot B12s were frequent visitors to Cambridge. Here no. 61535 arrives on shed for coaling and watering. B12s were mostly built at Stratford Works, with others by W. Beardmore & Co. and Beyer Peacock. No. 61535 was withdrawn in December 1959.

3.4.55

The summer weekends during the 1950s certainly kept Skegness station busy with excursions and specials, some from as far away as London, in addition to the usual service trains. Grantham B12 no. 61553 has just arrived and is waiting to move its stock into the sidings before its return journey.

19.6.55

# Chapter 2
# Mixed Traffic Locomotives

There are a great many designs in this section, among them the Thompson & Peppercorn A2 Pacifics mentioned earlier. One of the best known, principally designed for fast goods work, was the Gresley V2 class (classified 6MT), although right from their introduction in 1936 they could also be found on passenger work. These powerful locomotives, with their 6ft 2in driving wheels and 33,730lb tractive effort, were equally at home on principal expresses or on much more mundane work. During the Second World War V2s performed many Herculean haulage feats, in the process becoming renowned for their contribution to the war effort.

You would hardly expect a brand-new design to make its debut at the height of hostilities, but in 1942 the Thompson 5MT B1 class did just that. Even more remarkable was the fact that the engines were named. This was a highly successful design, the LNER equivalent of the famous LMS 'Black Fives', although the latter had 6ft driving wheels as opposed to the B1s' 6ft 2in ones. The B1 also had a slightly higher tractive effort.

Another class that was occasionally seen on the southern end of the East Coast main line was the B16, a North Eastern Railway design first introduced in 1920. In 1944 Edward Thompson commenced a programme of rebuilding these engines, after which they were classified B16/3. York members of the class were widely travelled and also regularly worked on the Great Central line.

Locomotives of the 2–6–0 wheel arrangement were commonplace. They included the Gresley K3s and a sole rebuild by Thompson in 1945, no. 61863, which became K5 class. Others included the earlier K2s and the K1s. The K2s, mostly named, will long be remembered for their work over the difficult West Highland line.

The three A2/2 4–6–2s allocated to New England were mostly used on semi-fast passenger services. One exception was the Sunday morning 9.16 a.m. local to Kings Cross, which was a regular duty for these engines at this time. Here no. 60505 *Thane of Fife* departs Huntingdon.                                                                                11.7.54

(*Opposite, top*): The six Gresley P2 class 2–8–2s were rebuilt in 1943–4 as Pacifics and classified A2/2. No. 60506 *Wolf of Badenoch* was one of three allocated to New England, the others being York engines. It is seen here leaving Huntingdon with the Sunday morning Kings Cross service. It was withdrawn in April 1961.                                                  10.1.54

(*Opposite, bottom*): The first A2/3 was no. 60500 *Edward Thompson*, completed at Doncaster in May 1946 and named after its designer. These engines had many innovations, including self-cleaning smokebox and steam brakes. No. 60500 is seen here at Huntingdon departing for Kings Cross. Note the plain chimney which was later replaced by a much more attractive lipped one.                                                                                          20.6.54

In the mid-1950s Haymarket depot had a sizeable number of Pacifics in its eighty-strong allocation, among them A2/3 no. 60519 *Honeyway*, seen here at Heaton depot. Note the old bent fire-irons and other tools lying around. Such clutter was by no means unusual at some sheds, while others were kept very tidy. 7.7.56

New England depot had nine Pacifics in its allocation, which were mainly used on semi-fast passenger services. One regular turn was the first London service on a Sunday morning. Here A2/3 no. 60513 *Dante* pulls away smartly from Huntingdon with a mid-week train. Built at Doncaster, it was completed in August 1946 and withdrawn in April 1963, having spent most of its working life at New England. 9.5.56

A2/3 no. 60515 *Sun Stream* was a North Eastern engine for its entire working life, Heaton, Gateshead and York being the only depots to which it was allocated. It was moved to York in December 1952 and remained there until withdrawal in November 1962.                    7.7.56

New England engines were regular visitors to York. Here A2/3 no. 60514 *Chamossaire* stands ready for its return working. The Thompson A2/3s, with one exception, continued the policy of naming locomotives after classic horse-race winners, in this case the 1945 St Leger.                    7.7.56

Among the Pacifics arriving on shed at Haymarket depot was A2/3 no. 60517 *Ocean Swell*, named after the 1944 Derby winner. This engine was fitted with a lipped chimney and was allocated to Heaton depot at this time.                                         21.8.55

(*Opposite, top*): Some of the A2s received a double chimney, but this was not the case with no. 60537 *Bachelor's Button* (named after the winner of the 1905 Doncaster Cup). When new, this engine was allocated first to Copley Hill and then New England, but in 1949 it moved north of the border, where it was to remain until withdrawal in December 1962. It is pictured here against the familiar Dundee background.                                         23.8.55

(*Opposite, bottom*): A2 no. 60525 *A.H. Peppercorn* was completed in December 1947, the month before nationalisation. Throughout its working life it never received a double chimney. It was only allocated to three depots, initially Doncaster, then New England, and finally Aberdeen in 1949; it remained at Aberdeen until withdrawal in March 1963. Unfortunately the light conditions were poor when this picture was taken at its home depot.                                         24.8.55

The A2/1 class consisted of just four engines, only one of which was to be found in the Eastern Region, the other three being in Scotland. No. 60508 *Duke of Rothesay* was allocated to New England. It is seen here leaving Sandy with a Peterborough semi-fast. 29.4.56

(*Opposite, top*): A2 no. 60533 *Happy Knight* pulls away from Huntingdon with the first Sunday Peterborough service. In its latter days this engine was allocated to New England. It was withdrawn in June 1963. 21.4.63

(*Opposite, bottom*): Doncaster V2 no. 60849 approaches Huntingdon with a mixed goods. The V2s were 'maids of all work', handling fast goods and heavy mineral trains, parcels, semi-fast and express passenger services. 2.10.55

I was lucky to see A2/3 no. 60500 *Edward Thompson* at Huntingdon heading a Kings Cross to Peterborough local, with V2 no. 60800 *Green Arrow* heading the afternoon pick-up goods. Both locomotives were the pioneers of their respective classes.  27.7.52

(*Opposite*): During the early 1950s some express trains changed engines at Peterborough. V2 no. 60912 has just taken over a heavy express. Starting off in wet greasy conditions could be difficult here as the station was on a curve. At this time C12 4–4–2Ts were used as bankers, creating quite startling sound effects as they blasted away under the overall roof.  5.9.53

V2 class locomotives had a long history on the East Coast main line and could be seen on anything from express passenger services to heavy coal trains. Here no. 60948, a New England engine, is seen in charge of a long train of articulated bolster wagons.                                                                                      28.3.63

The evening Kings Cross to Peterborough semi-fast was often worked by a V2, in this case no. 60914 of Kings Cross depot. Locomotives of this class were equally at home on principal express trains, semi-fasts, parcels and fitted goods. The Kings Cross V2s included the well-known pioneer engine no. 60800 *Green Arrow*, a very familiar sight throughout the 1950s.                                                                                          18.6.57

Fresh from general overhaul, V2 no. 60855 stands ready to return to its home shed, Heaton. Seventeen V2s were allocated to this depot in the mid-1950s, three of which were named; another twelve were based at Gateshead. In total 183 V2s were built; only one, no. 60800 *Green Arrow*, has survived into preservation. 7.7.56

Fresh from general overhaul at Darlington Works, V2 no. 60937 waits to move over to the running shed for steaming trials before returning to its home depot, St Margaret's. This engine was completed at Doncaster in March 1942 and was in service for over twenty years. 7.7.56

V2 no. 60959, one of a batch of seventeen allocated to St Margaret's depot, is seen here receiving attention from the shed staff. The V2s with their 33,730lb tractive effort were well liked by enginemen. This was considerably higher than that of the B1 4–6–0s and the Class 5s, both of which types were widely distributed in Scotland. The engine in the background is 'Scottish Director' no. 62677 *Eddie Ochiltree*. 22.8.55

Engines from the Newcastle sheds were daily visitors to Edinburgh. No. 60886 was a Heaton engine. It is seen here at St Margaret's awaiting its return working with another member of the class from south of the border. Note the two different types of tender fitted to the V2s. 21.8.55

Unquestionably one of Sir Nigel Gresley's finest designs was the V2 class 2–6–2. These powerful locomotives were equally at home on goods trains but were especially valuable for working fast goods, parcels and express passenger services. They had numerous haulage feats to their credit, especially during the war. No. 60915, seen here at Annesley, was one of six allocated to Woodford Halse depot.                                                                                     4.4.54

The fitting of Kylchap double-blast pipes and chimney to V2 no. 60880 in August 1961 certainly gave the locomotive a different appearance. Only eight members of the class were modified in this way, but despite the considerable improvements it brought, it was all too late in the day. No. 60880, seen here at Peterborough on stand-by duty, was withdrawn in September 1963.                                6.9.62

In the 1950s the Cleethorpes to Kings Cross service was worked by Immingham depot B1s. On very busy occasions a relief train would run in addition to the normal service. B1 no. 61409 is seen here at speed nearing Huntingdon on a relief. The Immingham B1s were later replaced by the Britannias, which took over from them in the 1960s. Both were kept in immaculate condition. 28.4.54

(*Opposite, top*): For a great many years the Peterborough to Kings Cross local services were in the hands of Great Northern Atlantics. By the 1950s these services were worked by B1 4–6–0s and L1 2–6–4 tanks allocated to Hitchin depot. Here B1 no. 61097 approaches Huntingdon with an evening service with a good head of steam, leaving a pall of smoke behind. 26.4.54

(*Opposite, bottom*): The decision to name thirty-nine members of the B1 class after types of antelope resulted in some very unusual locomotive names. One such was no. 61018 *Gnu*, one of the shortest names of any engine. This practice continued for the first forty locomotives, after which a few were named after LNER directors, with one exception, *Mayflower*. *Gnu* was completed at Darlington in February 1947 and remained in service until November 1965. It is seen here at York. 2.5.64

Low evening sunshine picks out the detail on B1 no. 61331 as it leaves Huntingdon with a semi-fast. Throughout the 1950s and into the early 1960s Kings Cross had nine B1s.                                                    9.61

The introduction of the B1 class in 1942, when the railways were already struggling to withstand the pressures generated by the war, was remarkable in itself. It was a brave decision by Edward Thompson, who had taken over as Chief Mechanical Engineer of the LNER. No. 61032 *Stembok* is pictured here at Stockton.
8.7.56

Self-weighing tenders enabled detailed results to be obtained on coal consumption. Here B1 no. 61140 is seen leaving Eastfield for its next duty. This engine was the first of a batch built in 1947 by the Vulcan Foundry and it remained in service until December 1966.
26.8.55

B1 no. 61095, a Lincoln engine, was photographed at a run-down March shed. Most of the locomotives to be seen here at this time, other than those already withdrawn, were visitors. No. 61095 was running with a self-weighing tender. This was academic, as coal consumption trials would not have been carried out at this time.
21.7.63

Another Stockton B1, no. 61019 *Nilghai*, is seen here in company with two veteran vehicles, part of a breakdown set. The B1s were mixed traffic locomotives, although they spent most of their time on passenger work. Unusually the Stockton engines were mostly used on goods duties.                                                                                                          8.7.56

On very rare occasions a Stockton B1 worked south of Peterborough. This always caused a bit of a stir, especially if it was a named engine. No. 61032 *Stembok* is seen here at its home shed. This engine was completed at Darlington in August 1947 and remained in service until November 1966. In total 410 B1s were built, one of which, no. 61057, was in service for just four years before being withdrawn after an accident.                                                                       8.7.56

Shortly after this picture of B1 no. 61300 was taken at March it was transferred to service stock for carriage heating. It was to remain on these duties until condemned in November 1965. No. 61300 was built by the North British Locomotive Company and completed in 1948.                                                                 23.6.63

For many years the Cambridge buffet trains were worked by 'Sandringhams' but by 1954 B1s were also frequently to be seen on these trains. Here no. 61287 stands in the bay awaiting departure time. Ten B1s were allocated to Cambridge and regularly worked trains to Liverpool Street and Kings Cross.                                           13.7.54

During the early 1960s a number of withdrawn engines were to be seen in the yards at March, along with others placed in store. Most would never work again. No. 61323 was transferred to service stock but promptly withdrawn, and it never did receive its departmental number.                                                                                            21.6.64

(*Opposite, top*): In the months immediately before closure March shed had a number of B1s stored in the yard, together with other locomotives either in store or already condemned. B1 no. 61181 could have been restored to service quickly if necessary. It was built by the Vulcan Foundry in 1947; withdrawal came in November 1963 when it was transferred to service stock for carriage heating. It became departmental no. 18 and was condemned in December 1965.                              9.63

(*Opposite, bottom*): In November 1963 March shed lost its few remaining steam locomotives, although for some time visiting engines still arrived. Also present were examples of the B1s allocated to service stock. No. 21, formerly no. 61233, is seen here. The couplings of these engines were removed so they could not be used other than for service purposes, although they were still capable of running light engine.                                                              21.6.64

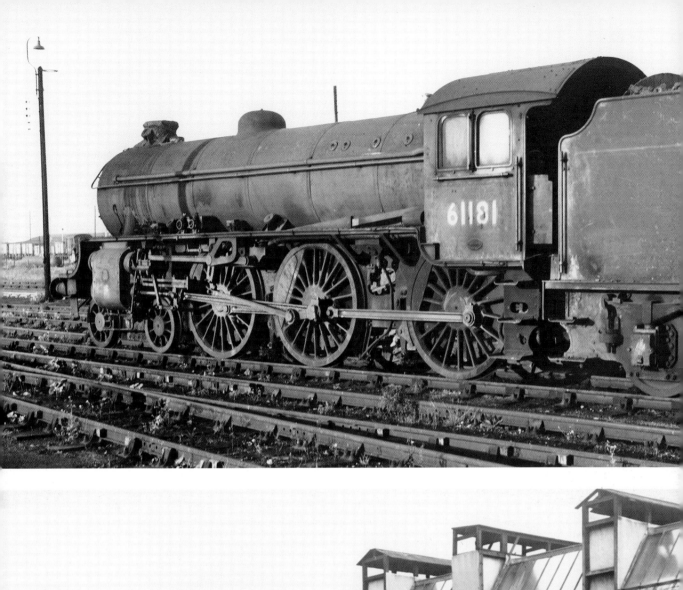

DEPARTMENTAL
LOCOMOTIVE
Nº 21

At least one B16 could usually be found at Annesley shed during the weekend. No. 61454, a B16/3 rebuild, was built at Darlington in October 1923. It was one of a sizeable number of the class allocated to York depot. The last example of this very useful design was withdrawn in July 1964.                                                                                                                4.4.54

B16/3 no. 61464 is seen here awaiting entry into Darlington Works. It was rebuilt in April 1945 and remained in service until September 1963. Signs of hard work can certainly be seen on the smokebox door.                                                          7.7.56

The B16/3s, including no. 61454, were rebuilds by Thompson, introduced in 1944 with three Walschaerts gears. Engines of this class could be found on duties that took them some distance from the North Eastern Region. In this case no. 61454 was photographed at Annesley. On a number of occasions I can recall B16s south of Peterborough, mostly on 'pigeon specials'.                                                                                                                                                4.4.54

B16/1 no. 61469, seen here at Heaton, was an example of the class introduced in 1919 with Stephenson gear; it was completed in December 1919 and never rebuilt. In 1949 it was allocated the new number 61400 but was renumbered 61469 in December of that year to free up the first number for a new B1. Withdrawal came in October 1960.                                7.7.56

York depot had a large allocation of B16s, which travelled far and wide. Destinations included Woodford Halse on the Great Central and even, at times, the East Coast main line south of Peterborough. No. 61419 (in un-rebuilt form) was constructed at Darlington in November 1920 and remained in service until September 1961.                    23.9.56

(*Opposite, top*): The B16s were very useful mixed traffic locomotives that were equally at home on goods and express passenger services. During the summer months they were often to be found heading excursion trains. No. 61433, seen here at Selby, was a Leeds Neville Hill engine. It had recently undergone a general overhaul. Built at Darlington in 1921, it completed thirty-eight years' service.                    23.9.56

(*Opposite, bottom*): The West Highland line presented several operating problems, not least its severe curves and long steep gradients. As a result the K4 class was introduced by Sir Nigel Gresley in 1937, with just six engines being constructed between 1937 and 1939. All were named, the first *Loch Long* and the other five after Scottish clan chiefs. No. 61998 *McLeod of McLeod* is seen here almost ready to leave Eastfield depot.                    26.8.55

K1 class no. 62020 rounds the curve at St Ives heading a mixed goods destined for March. Thirty K1s were allocated to 31B depot. No. 62020 was completed in 1949 by the North British Locomotive Company, which built all of the seventy-strong class in 1949–50. In addition there was also one K1/1, rebuilt in 1945 from a K4. No. 62020 was withdrawn in January 1965.                                                                                                    17.3.54

(*Opposite, top*): Stockton shed had a long association with the K1 design. No. 62064 is seen here outside the eight-road shed entrance. The class with the highest number of representatives here was the WD 2–8–0, with fifteen allocated in the early 1950s. By the end of the decade the depot's total stock had fallen from fifty-four to thirty-one, only six being WDs. The shed closed in June 1959, the remaining locomotives being transferred to Thornaby and Darlington.                8.7.56

(*Opposite, bottom*): March K1s were frequently seen at St Ives, and here no. 62036 heads a van train.                1.7.54

Locomotives fresh from overhaul at Doncaster Works were to be found at the motive power depot at weekends. After running-in trials, they would be sent back to their home shed. No. 62049 was a York engine, built in 1949 by the North British Locomotive Company.                                                                                                      10.11.54

(*Opposite, top*): Blaydon was also in the Gateshead district and was allocated the shedcode 52C. Most of its allocation consisted of goods or shunting locomotives, the exceptions being two D49s and a sizeable number of G5 0–4–4Ts. Throughout the 1950s Blaydon was home to a number of K1 class 2–6–0s, including no. 62002.                                  7.7.56

(*Opposite, bottom*): K1 no. 62039 heads a lightweight goods through St Ives. The station, which can be seen in the background, was on a tight curve. To the left of the signal-box was the line to Huntingdon used by the Cambridge–Kettering line trains.                                                                                                                          24.6.54

Although it was June a heavy sea mist shrouded Skegness when this picture of K2 no. 61745 was taken. Boston was the home shed of this locomotive, which had arrived with a service train. In keeping with former LNER practice, the class and shed details were stencilled on the buffer beam. Note also the interesting first coach.                                                                                                 19.6.55

The K2s will probably be best remembered for their work on the West Highland line. They were of course allocated to many other depots, not just in Scotland. No. 61754, seen here at Colwick, was one of the batch built by the North British Locomotive Company in 1918. Others were built at Doncaster and by Kitson & Company. This engine was withdrawn from service in December 1959.                    4.4.54

During the early 1950s a number of K2 class 2–6–0s were allocated to Stratford, including no. 61780, seen here at Cambridge. This engine was built by Kitson & Company in 1921, one of a sizeable batch. When this picture was taken it was still fitted with a Westinghouse pump, which was removed in 1955. Note the scorching on the smokebox door. 14.11.51

Kitson & Company built K2 no. 61776 in 1921. In November 1934 it received a side-window cab, and during November 1947 it was turned out in smart green livery, although this lasted only two years. In the mid-1950s Thornton Junction had two K2 class locomotives in its allocation. No. 61776, an Eastfield engine, was withdrawn in March 1959. 23.8.55

A visitor to Thornton Junction depot was K2 no. 61721, a Dunfermline engine built at Doncaster in 1913. This locomotive did not receive a side-window cab until November 1951. In the background is another Dunfermline engine, WD no. 90542.                                                                                                    23.8.55

(*Opposite, top*): Another of the K2s to be repainted in green livery was no. 61789 *Loch Laidon*, pictured here at Eastfield. The livery reverted to black when the engine received its BR number. No. 61789 was in the last batch of K2s built and was completed by Kitson & Company in August 1921. It remained in service until September 1959.          26.8.55

(*Opposite, bottom*): The K2s had a long history of working on the West Highland line, with members of the class allocated to Eastfield and Fort William in the mid-1950s. Those at Eastfield also worked elsewhere. No. 61764 *Loch Arkaig* is seen here at Eastfield in a far-from-ideal photographic location.                                  26.8.55

K2 no. 61781 *Loch Morar* was showing signs of hard work on its smokebox door. A dent was also visible on the front of the running plate. Eastfield had twelve K2s in its allocation, several of which were named.                                              26.8.55

(*Opposite, top*): By the mid-1950s most of the K2s were starting to show their age. This was certainly the case with no. 61794 *Loch Oich*. The smokebox door was badly scorched and considerable damage can be seen on the footplating. The whole engine was in a grubby condition.                                              26.8.55

(*Opposite, bottom*): When I set out on my Scottish trip in 1955 one of the classes I particularly wanted to photograph was the V4 2–6–2. Only two of these were built, both at Doncaster in 1941. They were allocated to Aberdeen Ferryhill in 1954. Unfortunately no. 61700 *Bantam Cock* was at work, and sister engine no. 61701, not officially named but often referred to as *Bantam Hen*, was not in the best location for photography.                                              24.8.55

During the early 1950s one subject that I photographed on several occasions was a Sunday fish train hauled by an Immingham depot K3. It usually passed Huntingdon at about 9 a.m., sometimes after the London semi-fast, or, as on this occasion, before it – hence it was being turned slow road. No. 61825 was in immaculate condition. The passing of this train left you in no doubt about the vans' contents!                                                                                              9.5.54

(*Opposite, top*): The K3s were easily recognisable by the large-diameter boiler. Classified 6MT, they were widely used on passenger services. The arrival of B1 4–6–0s resulted in them being mostly employed on goods work. No. 61980, seen here at Annesley, was a Darlington-built engine which entered service in December 1936.                                    4.4.54

(*Opposite, bottom*): This picture of K3 no. 61975 at Annesley has been included as it shows clearly the single vacuum reservoir on the tender. This engine was built at Darlington and completed in November 1936. Withdrawal came in September 1961. Note the old coach body in use as a store or mess room.                                                              4.4.54

The only examples of the K3 class to be found in Scotland in the mid-1950s were at St Margaret's, which had twenty-three, including no. 61924, seen here at Perth. This engine was built by Armstrong Whitworth in 1934 and remained in service until November 1960.        25.8.55

March had a considerable number of 2–6–0s in its allocation, comprising both K1 2–6–0s introduced in 1949 and the Gresley K3 class. Here no. 61943 rounds the curve at Meadow Lane crossing, St Ives, on its way to London with a mixed goods.        17.3.54.

Considerable amounts of goods traffic daily used the March to Cambridge line, known as the 'St Ives loop'. K3 no. 61946 heads a mixed freight at St Ives. This engine was built by the North British Locomotive Company and completed in September 1935. It is fitted with the 4,200-gallon group standard tender. 1.7.54

The afternoon March parcels train was worked by a variety of locomotives, with 'Sandringhams', 'Clauds' and K3s all commonly seen. K3 no. 61886 is seen here nearing St Ives, where the station staff would be ready and waiting. 1.7.54

The once-busy yards of March depot contained many stored locomotives. Here K3 no. 61942 awaits its final journey. March had a long association with K3s and the Peppercorn K1s. No. 61942 had already been withdrawn for eight months when this picture was taken. 26.5.63

In June 1945 Edward Thompson took the decision to rebuild K3 LNER no. 206 with two cylinders and a boiler pressure of 225lb (as opposed to the 180lb of the K3s). The rebuild was eventually classified K5 and ran as no. 61863. Despite its success, no more locomotives were rebuilt in this way. No. 61863 is seen here at Stratford. It remained in service until June 1960. 7.5.55

# Chapter 3
# Freight Locomotives

These less glamorous but equally important engines quietly went about their business – although not so quietly when called upon to handle a particularly heavy train with the gradient against them. The majority of heavy haulage locomotives were eight-coupled designs and therefore lie beyond the scope of this book, but those with six-coupled driving wheels were of course the principal goods engines in their heyday. As larger and more powerful designs became available to handle the steadily increasing traffic, the six-coupled locomotives were generally restricted to pick-up and local goods workings.

Many of these engines were steam brake only, but one class that did include a few examples equipped for passenger train working was the ex-Great Eastern Railway J15. Cambridge had a number of these, and their duties included the Mildenhall branch, the Colne Valley line and one working that took them into London Midland territory. This was the first departure of the day from Cambridge and the last from Kettering. It was worked by a J15 classified 2F. The line had weak wooden trestle bridges between Huntingdon and St Ives and was also steeply graded nearer Kettering. Despite their increasing age, the J15s were sturdy, powerful and reliable locomotives. The Great Eastern Railway certainly recognised their virtues, and built them in large numbers.

There were many other 0–6–0 designs. Some of North Eastern Railway origin spent their entire working lives handling coal and mineral traffic in the north-east, while others worked the difficult trans-Pennine route to Penrith. The Great Central and North British Railways also contributed a considerable number of 0–6–0s, many of which were to pass into BR ownership.

Hitchin shed had one example of the J1 class in its allocation. Its usual duties were engineers' trains, as seen here at Huntingdon. In its final years it was occasionally called upon to take on Herculean tasks, once working a fourteen-coach Leeds express through to Kings Cross. This was not the only time the J1 found itself in charge of an express. Locomotive shortages often resulted in it working local passenger trains from Hitchin to Kings Cross and return. No. 65013 was the last survivor of its class, being withdrawn in November 1954.                                                 9.9.54

The J2 class was introduced by Ivatt to work fast goods traffic on the East Coast main line. Ten were built at Doncaster in 1912. No. 65023 is seen here ex-works at Lincoln. Nine J2s passed into British Railways ownership. No. 65023 was withdrawn in November 1953, with the last J2 going in the following year.   26.8.51

This might have been 'the one that got away'. My attention was drawn to a train on the Up line, but I turned to find J4 no. 64112 quietly heading an engineers' train on the main line. Built at Doncaster in 1896, it must have been making one of its final trips south of Peterborough as it was withdrawn in December 1951.                                        6.10.51

In the early 1950s New England depot had a number of veteran ex-Great Northern Railway 0–6–0s in its allocation, among them J3 class no. 64131, built at Doncaster in 1898. It started out as a J4, was rebuilt in January 1924 and was withdrawn in December 1954. It is seen here fitted with a J6-type chimney. 28.1.51

Time was running out for J5 no. 65494, seen here at Colwick. When this picture was taken only nine of the twenty-strong class remained in service, the last being withdrawn in December 1955. Introduced for heavy goods workings, the J5s were occasionally seen on passenger trains but only in the summer months, as they were not fitted for steam heating. No. 65494 was completed at Doncaster in December 1909 and withdrawn in January 1955. 4.4.54

For several years a pick-up goods ran in the early evening from Huntingdon to Hitchin. The usual motive power was a J6, although Fowler 2–6–4Ts also appeared for a short period when allocated to Hitchin. Here no. 64186 stands ready to commence its return journey. 20.4.55

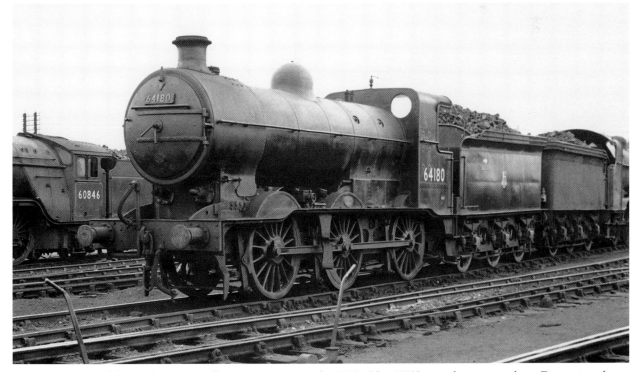

Many examples of the J6 class were still going strong into the 1960s. No. 64180, seen here ex-works at Doncaster after a general overhaul, remained in service until March 1960, but it wasn't until June 1962 that the last survivors were withdrawn. As with many ex-Great Northern Railway locomotives, the J6s had brass works plates; the one on no. 64180 can be seen on the middle splasher. 23.9.56

Hitchin depot's J6 no. 64197 stands near Offord with a Sunday engineers' train. At this time track was mostly laid in lengths, and some of these can be seen on the flat wagons. In their final years the J6 class engines were employed on local goods, trip working and engineers' trains. 2.10.55

(*Opposite, top*): Many veteran coaches were still in use during the 1950s but for very different purposes from those they were built for. This six-wheel coach, no. 940467, photographed at Huntingdon, was used as a ballast brake van and was allocated to Peterborough District Engineers. J6 no. 64279 was one of a large number of this class allocated to New England, where their duties included working engineers' trains. 10.3.54

(*Opposite, bottom*): Withdrawals of the J6 class did not begin until the mid-1950s, with a fair number of the 110-strong design surviving into the 1960s. No. 64199, photographed at Colwick, was completed at Doncaster in May 1913 and withdrawn in April 1958. The spartan cab conditions of these engines can be clearly seen in this picture. 4.4.54

E940467
BALLAST BRAKE VAN
PETERBOROUGH DISTRICT
KSTORS

64279

64199

The J6s were very versatile locomotives, equally at home on goods or passenger trains, and were capable of a fair turn of speed. The entire class, all built at Doncaster between 1911 and 1922, were fitted with vacuum brakes. One of the largest concentrations of these engines was at New England, where no. 64224, seen here at Huntingdon, was allocated. During the 1950s they were an almost daily sight on engineers' trains, which usually included at least one veteran coach.    9.5.54

At large depots it was well worth keeping an eye on what the shed pilot was doing. Often, as locomotives were marshalled ready for their next duty, something of particular interest would be pulled out of the shed. J10 no. 65153 was pilot at Trafford Park when this picture was taken.    16.10.55

One of the J10s to end its days at Darlington shed was no. 65181. Completed in June 1901, this was a Gorton-built engine. The tender was fitted with a weatherboard, and the engine with what was known as a flowerpot chimney. Several J10s were to be found at Trafford Park in the mid-1950s.                                                         16.10.55

In total seventy-eight J10s passed into British Railways ownership, although withdrawals had commenced as early as 1933. No. 65153, seen here at Trafford Park, was built by Beyer Peacock and completed in December 1926. In 1956 no. 65153 was among eight members of the class transferred to Darlington. They were not well received and did little work; all were withdrawn in December 1956.                                                                                16.10.55

Several private companies and Gorton Works were involved in the construction of the J11 class for the Great Central Railway. No. 64292, seen here at Annesley depot, was built by Neilson, Reid and completed in December 1901. Eighteen J11s were to see service in France during the First World War. These engines were equally at home on goods or passenger work and were highly regarded by enginemen. Withdrawals commenced in 1954 but it was not until the late 1950s that considerable inroads were made; the last was withdrawn in October 1962.                4.4.54

(*Opposite, top*): During the early 1950s the afternoon goods from St Ives to Huntingdon normally consisted of around twenty wagons. On arrival these would be shunted and sorted for forwarding to their destinations via the East Coast main line. Here no. 65474 arrives at Huntingdon East. Next to the locomotive is a flat wagon loaded with agricultural machinery.                16.3.54

(*Opposite, bottom*): The duties of the Huntingdon pilot included moving tank wagons as required by the fuel depots situated to the north of Huntingdon station. J15 no. 65461, fitted with Westinghouse brake and vacuum ejector, was one of the Cambridge locomotives of this class equipped to work passenger stock.                10.3.54

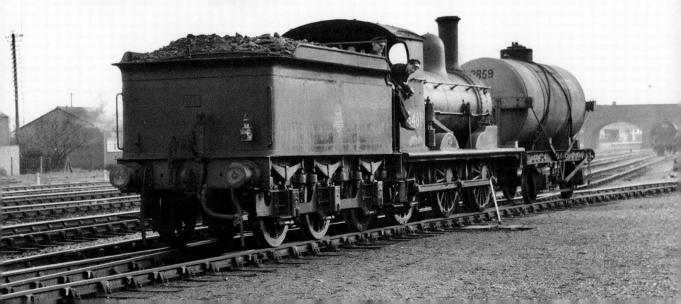

Only on rare occasions was J15 no. 65420 sent to Huntingdon on pilot duty. This engine was one of those fitted with steam brake only. The chimney still has the rim of a spark arrester fitted. In the early 1960s this J15 was used to lift track on the Kettering line. Every night the engine returned to New England for servicing.          14.6.56

(*Opposite, top*): It was unusual for a Bury St Edmunds J15 to be sent on the ten-day roster to Huntingdon sub-shed. No. 65391 was fitted with a side-window cab. This engine was completed at Stratford Works in October 1890 and withdrawn in 1958, after an amazing sixty-eight years' service! This picture was taken at Huntingdon East station.  27.7.51

(*Opposite, bottom*): One of the last J15s in service was no. 65420, which used to work trains involved in branch line lifting in East Anglia. It spent some time on the St Ives–Kettering line, travelling daily between New England and Huntingdon. Its day's work over, it is seen here running to Peterborough coupled to a passing WD.          21.9.61

The Mildenhall branch services were a regular duty for Cambridge depot. J15 no. 65451 had arrived with the afternoon train and was being turned ready for the journey back. The enginemen were keen to get this job done as they then had some spare time before the return journey.                                                                                            31.5.56

(*Opposite, top*): One of the Cambridge J15s was sent to Huntingdon on a ten-day roster for pilot duty. This involved shunting and working a local goods service to St Ives. Up until the early 1950s the locomotive also ran a two-coach passenger service to St Ives in the morning and evening. No. 65474 is seen here in Huntingdon yards before it moved over to the small sub-shed.                                                                                            6.8.54

(*Opposite, bottom*): Mildenhall was typical of many branch line stations in the 1950s. Here J15 no. 65451 stands ready to return to Cambridge. Ten J15s were allocated to 31A at the time, including no. 65390, a regular engine on the Kettering turn. Another was the Huntingdon pilot, while the remainder worked on various branch and station pilot duties.  31.5.56

All traces of this railway scene at St Ives in Cambridgeshire have long since disappeared. Here J15 no. 65461 has just finished shunting in the goods yard as K1 no. 62053 passes on its way to March with coal empties. The line between Cambridge and March was extensively used for freight traffic. 2.5.53

(*Opposite, top*): For a number of years the first train of the day from Cambridge to Kettering was a J15 turn. No. 65390, seen here nearing Godmanchester, was a regular engine on this duty. The locomotive returned with the last train from Kettering, and during the long stop-over it was often used as shed pilot. 5.7.54

(*Opposite, bottom*): J17 no. 65501 makes a gentle start from a siding at St Ives with a fruit train from March. This engine was allocated to King's Lynn and had steam brake only. Completed at Stratford in September 1900 as class J16, it was rebuilt to J17 in April 1929. It is seen here with a small tender. This engine was withdrawn in January 1958. 24.6.54

Fresh from a general overhaul at Stratford Works, J17 no. 65584 had been coaled and watered ready to return to its home depot. The locomotive is fitted with tablet exchange apparatus, which can be seen near the front tender handrail. Built in November 1910, no. 65584 remained in service until February 1960.                                                                 3.4.55

The afternoon parcels train arrives at St Ives with J17 no. 65580 in charge. The loading of this train varied considerably, especially in the summer months when large amounts of fruit from the area was carried. The train was worked by either Cambridge or March engines; no. 65580 was allocated to the former.                                                                 28.8.54

Seen here at Cambridge yard, J17 no. 65500 started life as a J16 class and was the first to be completed at Stratford Works in September 1900. Rebuilt to J17 in May 1929, it remained steam brake only throughout its working life.                                                                              26.2.56

Five J17 class locomotives were fitted with back cabs for goods workings on two East Anglian branches. No. 65575, seen here shunting at St Ives, received a tender cab in October 1952. It was allocated to Cambridge depot for a number of years and was withdrawn from service in February 1958.        17.3.54

J17 no. 65582 awaits its final journey at March shed. When this picture was taken the engine had already been condemned for eight months, although its tender was still fully coaled. The chimney had been protected in the customary way with a piece of tarpaulin. After being placed in store this engine, like so many others, never worked again.     26.5.63

(*Opposite, top*): J17 no. 65541 had been in use as a stationary boiler before it was condemned in September 1962. It had been moved to the sidings along with other withdrawn locomotives. It was in a poor state: the dome was loose on the boiler and one buffer was missing, as was the front coupling.     23.6.63

(*Opposite, bottom*): RCTS 'Fensman', seen here at Ramsey East, ready to work back to Somersham and rejoin the March–St Ives line. Only seventeen members of the class were fitted with vacuum ejectors and steam heat connections to enable them to work passenger trains, no. 65562 being modified in this way in May 1944. The engine remained in service until August 1958.     24.7.55

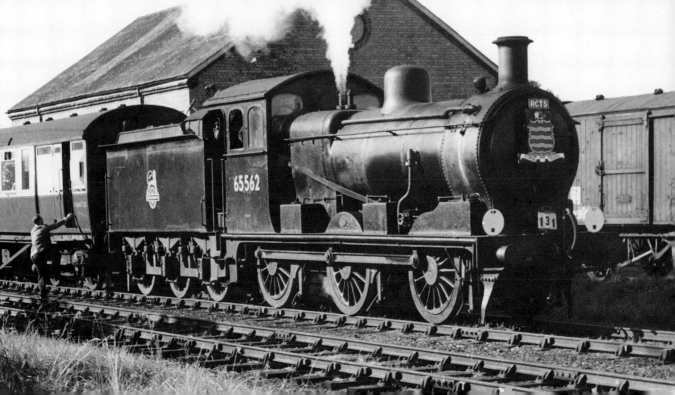

J19 no. 64671 pulls away from St Ives with a mixed goods on its way to March. Locomotives of this class were first introduced in 1912, and subsequent rebuilding with round-topped boilers and new chimneys gave them a more modern appearance. No. 64671 remained in service until February 1962.                                                   2.5.53

(*Opposite, top*): Over the years the Great Eastern Railway introduced a number of 0–6–0 designs, the J20s being the last of the line. These locomotives were widely regarded as the most powerful 0–6–0s in Britain until the Bulleid Q1 Austerity class appeared. No. 64699 was the last example built, entering service in January 1923. After several months in store at March depot, it was withdrawn in September 1962.                                                   21.7.63

(*Opposite, bottom*): The most numerous class of North Eastern 0–6–0s were the J21s, built between 1886 and 1895 and eventually totalling 201. Principally intended for goods working, they were also frequently used on passenger trains. Construction took place at Darlington and Gateshead. No. 65064 was built at the latter; it was completed in October 1890 and remained in service until September 1958.                                                   8.7.56

The North Eastern Railway J21 class was very similar in appearance to the Great Eastern J15; both were designed by T.W. Worsdell. The J21s were more powerful and were fitted with larger driving wheels. No. 65070 was photographed at Blaydon shed. Built at Darlington in 1891, it remained in service until May 1960, a remarkable sixty-nine years' service.    7.7.56

(*Opposite, top*): Had it not been for the Second World War J21 no. 65061 would, in all probability, have been withdrawn in the late 1930s or early 1940s. Instead in 1939 it was reinstated and remained in service until May 1958. It is seen here at Blaydon.    7.7.56

(*Opposite, bottom*): The J25 class was introduced in 1898 by W. Worsdell, and a total of 120 were built over a four-year period from 1898 to 1902. Some seventy-six were taken into British Railways stock, with a number being withdrawn shortly afterwards. Pictured at Tyne Dock, no. 65670 was built at Gateshead Works in 1899. In 1939 it was placed in store, but at the start of the war it was returned to traffic and remained in service until June 1962.    7.7.56

J25 no. 65685, seen here at York, was completed at Darlington in December 1899. It was a steam brake saturated engine with slide valves. It was withdrawn in September 1959 after completing almost sixty years' service.          23.9.56

(*Opposite, top*): In their early days the J25 locomotives were responsible for heavy goods traffic but by the 1950s they were employed on local goods and trip workings. No. 65717, seen here at Tyne Dock, was built at Gateshead Works in 1902 and remained in service until October 1958.          7.7.56

(*Opposite, bottom*): There were two types of cab spectacles fitted to the J26 class. No. 65740, seen here, has the shaped design. This engine was built at Darlington in 1904 and remained in service until January 1959. Signs of hard work can be clearly seen on the smokebox in this picture, taken at Newport.          8.7.56

All fifty J26 0–6–0s were fitted with steam brakes and three-link couplings. Initially these locomotives were mostly employed on long-distance work but with the arrival of more powerful engines, their duties were largely restricted to mineral trains. Nevertheless all fifty survived to be taken into British Railways stock, the first withdrawals taking place in the late 1950s. No. 65740 was photographed at Newport, Co. Durham.                                         8.7.56

(*Opposite, top*): Fresh from works overhaul, J27 no. 65805 had just arrived back at its home depot, Haverton Hill. This class consisted of 115 locomotives, 10 of which were built in LNER days between 1906 and 1923. The majority, including no. 65805, were constructed at Darlington. Three private companies also built batches; these were the North British Locomotive Company, Beyer Peacock and Robert Stephenson. No. 65805 had a long working life; completed in September 1908, it remained in service until January 1966.                                         8.7.56

(*Opposite, bottom*): York was the final depot to which J27 no. 65894 was allocated. Constructed at Darlington in September 1923, it was the last of the class to be built. Both the J27s standing in the depot yard were in good external condition at a time when dirt and grime was commonplace.                                         23.9.56

It was unusual for depots to be allocated just one class of locomotive but this was the case at Percy Main, where throughout the 1950s more than twenty J27s were allocated. Here nos 65831 and 65852 await their next turn of duty.  7.7.56

J27 no. 65876 was an example of the class with piston valves. The J27s were the true workhorses of the North Eastern Region, handling a considerable amount of coal traffic during the 1950s and 1960s. No. 65876 was photographed at Blaydon depot.
                                                                                                          7.7.56

In their heyday the J35 class 0–6–0s could be seen on heavy goods trains and occasionally on local passenger duties. By the 1950s they were to be found on much more mundane tasks. No. 64462 is seen here at St Margaret's. This engine was among the first of the class to be built, being completed in 1900 by the North British Locomotive Company. 21.8.55

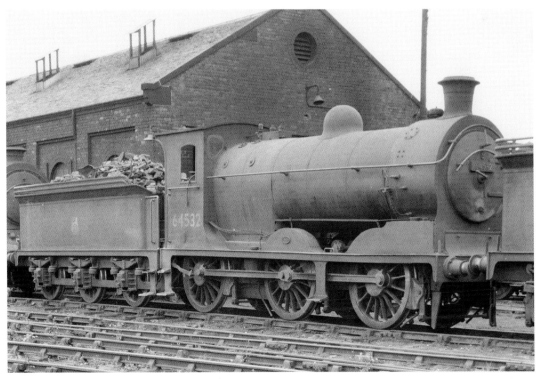

In all seventy members of the J35 class were taken into British Railways stock, five having been withdrawn in 1946–7. It was to be another eleven years before any further withdrawals took place, and the last example was condemned in 1962. No. 64532 is seen here at St Margaret's depot; engines from here were to be found at many sub-sheds in the Edinburgh area. 21.8.55

J35 no. 64506 stands over the ashpits at Thornton Junction depot. The massive coaling plant can be seen in the background. Also in the picture is 'Scott' no. 62429 *The Abbot*. Thornton, with an allocation of 107 locomotives, was the principal shed of the 62A district.                                                                                          23.8.55

(*Opposite, top*): The ex-North British Railway Thornton Junction depot, with its spacious yards, was a good place for photography, unlike many depots where the lines were tightly packed together and festooned with posts and poles. Here J35 no. 64522 fills its tender, having already coaled up for its next duty.                                                 23.8.55

(*Opposite, bottom*): J35 no. 64482 stands on the turntable at Aberdeen Kittybrewster, with the shed building in the background. Built at Cowlairs Works, this engine was completed in December 1908. These very useful engines had long working lives; this example completed fifty-three years' service.                                                            24.8.55

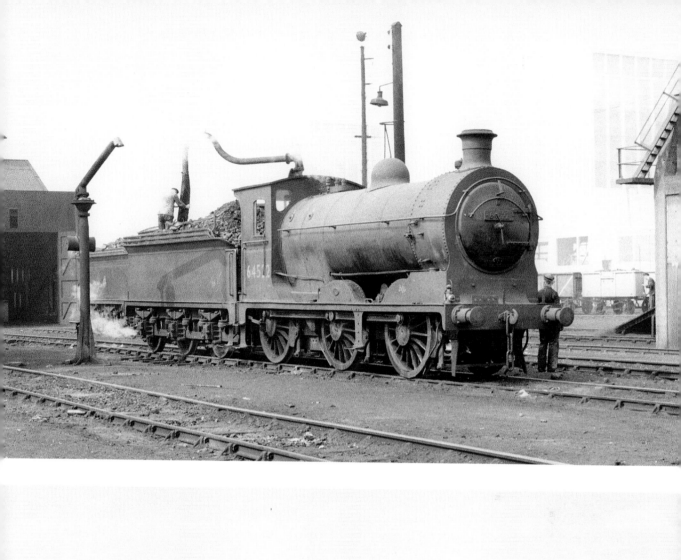

Locomotives allocated to Bathgate were only seen at Aberdeen Kittybrewster on the way to or from Inverurie Works. No. 64529 was completed in December 1912. In the mid-1950s only one example of the ex-North British Railway J35s was allocated to the depot.                    24.8.55

The locomotive depot at Aberdeen Kittybrewster was of Great North of Scotland Railway origin and was the principal shed of the district. The building was of an interesting half-roundhouse type. Here J35 no. 64482 stands in the yard with the massive coaling plant in the background. Presumably the number 6 on the tender refers to a duty number.                    24.8.55

After a general overhaul, J35/5 was en route from Inverurie to its home depot, Hawick, having called at Dundee for coal and water. No. 64463 was one of the class with piston valves. 23.8.55

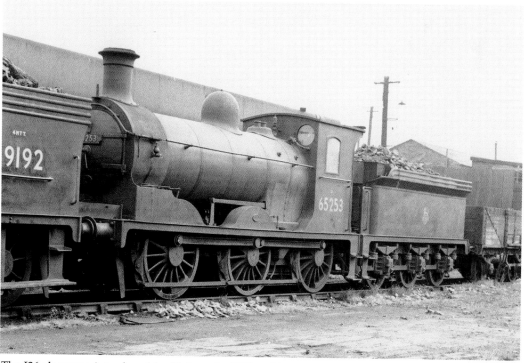

The J36 class was introduced by Holmes in 1888 and in 1917 twenty-five members of the class were commandeered by the government and dispatched to France to operate supply trains on the Western Front. No. 65253 *Joffe* went to the War Department in November 1917 and returned in May 1919. In recognition of their wartime service these engines were all given appropriate names, which were hand-painted on the middle splasher above the workplate. In the case of no. 65253, seen here at Dunfermline, this name was removed in 1954. 23.8.55

The North British Railway had a considerable number of 0–6–0s in its locomotive stock. On the right is J36 no. 65329, built at Cowlairs in 1900. The other engine is J37 no. 64608, built by the North British Locomotive Company in 1919. The J37 class was introduced by Reid in 1914.                                                                                              21.8.55

The first of the J36 class locomotives was completed at Cowlairs Works in August 1888, with the last of the 168-strong class being completed in December 1900. No. 65339, built in 1900 and seen here at Eastfield, was withdrawn in March 1961.                                                                                              26.8.55

The first J36 withdrawals came as early as 1926, but 123 passed into British Railways ownership. During their long working life they were to be found at all the North British Railway depots, where they were highly regarded by enginemen. No. 65309, seen here at Dundee, was built at Cowlairs in January 1889 and completed sixty-five years' service.  23.8.55

St Margaret's sub-shed Seafield was best visited on a Sunday when the majority of locomotives were present. In this picture are three J37s, with no. 64614 the most prominent; also present is a J35 class 0–6–0.  21.8.55

Fresh from what was almost certainly its last general overhaul, J37 no. 64538 is seen here at Seafield. It certainly stood out among the other work-stained members of the class. The J37s were the last of a series of 0–6–0 designs introduced by the North British Railway; it was a powerful design and popular with enginemen.                                21.8.55

Seafield was a sub-shed of St Margaret's. Most of the engines to be found there in the 1950s were J37 class 0–6–0s, two of which are seen here. Nos 64537 and 64577 were both built at Cowlairs Works. The North British Locomotive Company was also involved in the construction of this class.                                21.8.55

Several of Polmont depot's J37s were undergoing repairs at the time of my visit. No. 64636 had just had its front set of driving wheels removed with the aid of the depot breakdown crane, just visible in this picture. In this condition it was likely that some strain would be put on the engine's frames.      22.8.5

At the back of the Polmont shed building was another J37 undergoing repair. No. 64571's tender had been removed, and the coupling rods and other parts dismantled. Another J37 stands in the background, waiting for the shed's fitters.      22.8.55

Perth was a famous Caledonian Railway depot. During the mid-1950s the majority of its allocation was made up of former LMS engines, with just a small number being ex-LNER, although the latter were frequent daily visitors. J37 no. 64581 was an Eastfield locomotive that had worked in from Glasgow.                    26.8.55

(*Opposite, top*): Thornton Junction, with its nearby collieries, relied upon the J37 class 0–6–0s and WD 2–8–0s to work the coal traffic. No. 64576, seen here with other members of the class, was built by the North British Locomotive Company in 1918.                    23.8.55

(*Opposite, bottom*): The J37 class consisted of 104 locomotives built between 1914 and 1921; all except three were taken into British Railways stock and survived into the 1960s. No. 64576 was one of a number allocated to Thornton Junction. The J37s were a development of the J35 class.                    23.8.55

Thornton Junction was one of the largest Scottish Region depots and its allocation included a sizeable number of J37 0–6–0s, no. 64596 being one of them. In the background is one of the depot's seven B1s. Other locomotives present at the time of my visits were 4–4–0s of the 'Scots', 'Glens', 'Scottish Directors' and 'Hunts' classes.          23.8.55

During the 1950s Eastfield was one of the best of the Scottish Region depots to visit. Its allocation of 139 locomotives included examples of many different classes. J37 no. 64611 was one of seventeen members in the class allocated to Eastfield.          26.8.55

In the 1950s the Gresley J38 class were all to be found at Scottish depots, where their principal duties were main line goods and mineral trains. No. 65917 is seen here at Polmont, which had two members of the thirty-five-strong design in its allocation. They were all built at Darlington in 1926.  21.8.55

Two J38 0–6–0s gained the distinction of being the last Gresley-designed engines to be withdrawn from service. The J38s first made their appearance in 1926, with the entire class of thirty-five being built at Darlington in that year. They were very similar in appearance to the much more numerous J39s, but with smaller driving wheels: 4ft 8in, as opposed to the J39s' 5ft 2in. No. 65912 is seen here at St Margaret's.  21.8.55

Thornton Junction had a small repair shop incorporated in the shed buildings. At the time of my visit it was being kept busy. J38 no. 65910 appears to have suffered damage to its wheel bearings. Also in the row is a J37 and a 'Glen' 4–4–0, the tender of which is just visible.                                                                                                                    23.8.55

(*Opposite, top*): Eleven J38 0–6–0s were allocated to Dunfermline (Upper) depot, including no. 65933. Also in the picture is a veteran coach that was used with the shed's breakdown set. During the mid-1950s Dunfermline had an allocation of sixty-nine locomotives, which had reduced to fifty-four by the end of the decade.                                                               23.8.55

(*Opposite, bottom*): In total 289 J39 class locomotives were built between 1926 and 1941. The Eastern Region had the majority of them, with a sizeable number in the North Eastern Region and twenty-four in the Scottish Region. During the 1950s they were rare visitors south of Peterborough, although before that date they were frequently to be seen. No. 64860, seen here at Selby, was completed at Darlington in October 1935 and fitted with a 3500-gallon tender. While primarily goods locomotives, J39s were also seen on passenger work, especially excursions.                                         23.9.56

Only a small number of J39s were to be found in the Scottish Region, unlike the J38s, which were all based north of the border. No. 64866 is seen here at Eastfield. 26.8.55

Construction of the J39 class took place over a fifteen-year period, during which time changes were made to the design. No. 64980, seen here at Annesley, entered traffic from Darlington in May 1941. When complete, the class comprised 289 locomotives. 4.4.54